LIVING GREEN

Oceans, Islands, and Polar Regions

WORLD
BOOK

a Scott Fetzer company
Chicago
www.worldbookonline.com

Editorial:

Editor in Chief: Paul A. Kobasa
Project Manager: Cassie Mayer
Writer: Edward R. Ricciuti
Editors: Daniel Kenis, Brian Johnson
Researchers: Daniel Kenis, Cheryl Graham
Manager, Contracts & Compliance
  (Rights & Permissions): Loranne K. Shields
Indexer: David Pofelski

Graphics and Design:

Associate Director: Sandra M. Dyrlund
Associate Manager, Design: Brenda B. Tropinski
Associate Manager, Photography: Tom Evans
Book design by: Don Di Sante
Designer: Matthew Carrington
Contributing Photographs Editor: Carol Parden
Senior Cartographer: John Rejba

Pre-Press and Manufacturing:

Director: Carma Fazio
Manufacturing Manager: Steve Hueppchen
Production/Technology Manager: Anne Fritzinger

World Book, Inc.
233 N. Michigan Avenue
Chicago, IL 60601
U.S.A.

For information about other World Book publications, visit our Web site at **http://www.worldbookonline.com** or call **1-800-WORLDBK (967-5325)**.

For information about sales to schools and libraries, call **1-800-975-3250 (United States)**, or **1-800-837-5365 (Canada)**.

Picture Acknowledgments:

Front Cover: © JTB Photo Communications/Alamy Images

© All Canada Photos/Alamy Images 40; © Blickwinkel/Alamy Images 8, 10, 43; © Bryan & Cherry Alexander Photography/Alamy Images 47, 53; © Scott Camazine, Alamy Images 43; © Keren Su, China Span/Alamy Images 31; © Brandon Cole, Alamy Images 14, 15, 41; © Mark Conlin, Alamy Images 11; © Dennis Cox, Alamy Images 48; © dbimages/Alamy Images 20; © Danita Delimont, Alamy Images 35; © Reinhard Dirscherl, Alamy Images 13; © Thomas R. Fletcher, Alamy Images 32; © FLPA/Alamy Images 21; © Stephen Frink, Alamy Images 11; © Images&Stories/Alamy Images 24; © Steven J. Kazlowski, Alamy Images 44, 45; © Paul Andrew Lawrence, Alamy Images 52; © Neil McAllister, Alamy Images 23; © Megapress/Alamy Images 55; © Renee Morris, Alamy Images 29; © Galen Rowell, Mountain Light/Alamy Images 41; © nagelestock/Alamy Images 5; © Michael Patrick O'Neill, Alamy Images 17; © Nic Miller, Organics Image Library/Alamy Images 1; © Phototake/Alamy Images 25; © Robert Harding Picture Library/Alamy Images 28, 42; © Friedrich Stark, Alamy Images 45; © Visual&Written SL/Alamy Images 12; © Nik Wheeler, Alamy Images 26; AP/Wide World 34, 51, 54; © Ragnar Th. Sigurosson, Arctic-Images 27; © Getty Images 20; © Natalie Fobes, NGS Images/Getty Images 22; © Reuters/Landov 37; The Global Multi-Resolution Topography (GMRT) Synthesis/Marine Geoscience Data System (geomapapp.org) 18; © Masterfile 58; © Steve Haddock, MBARI 19; © Flip Nicklin, NMFS permit #987/Minden Pictures 17; NASA 4, 46; Northrop Grumman Corporation 55; © Fletcher & Baylis, Photo Researchers 29; © John Mitchell, Photo Researchers 33; © Michael Ord, Photo Researchers 30; © Doc White, SeaPics.com 50; © Shutterstock 7, 15, 16, 38, 56, 58, 59; © Mauritius/SuperStock 49; University of Washington 19; Glacier National Park Archives/Karen Holtzer, U.S. Geological Survey 57.

All maps and illustrations are the exclusive property of World Book, Inc.

Library of Congress Cataloging-in-Publication Data

Oceans, islands, and polar regions.
    p. cm. — (Living green)
  Includes bibliographical references and index.
  Summary: "General overview of ocean, island, and polar region ecosystems, including an exploration of disturbances these ecosystems face due to human interference, pollution, and climate change, and current conservation and reclamation efforts. Features include fact boxes, glossary, list of recommended reading and web sites, and index"—Provided by publisher.
  ISBN 978-0-7166-1402-9
  1. Marine ecology—Juvenile literature. 2. Island ecology—Juvenile literature. 3. Ecology—Polar regions—Juvenile literature. I. World Book, Inc.
QH541.5.S3O24 2009
577.7—dc22

2008022795

Living Green
Set ISBN: 978-0-7166-1400-5
Printed in Mexico
1 2 3 4 5 12 11 10 09 08

The text paper of this book contains a minimum of 10% post-consumer recovered fiber.

Table of Contents

There is a glossary of terms on pages 60-61. Terms defined in the glossary are in type **that looks like this** on their first appearance in any section.

Introduction

Section Summary

Oceans, islands, and polar regions are highly connected to one another. When any one of these ecosystems is affected by environmental change, the others are affected as well.

Human activities are disrupting the ecological balance of oceans, islands, and polar regions. Global warming, which is caused mainly by human activities, is one of the largest threats to these ecosystems. Global warming may cause great human suffering, too.

The crew of Apollo 17 took this photograph, known as the Blue Marble, in 1972.

Less than 100 years ago, humans had never seen what Earth looked like from space. The first images of our planet viewed from space were taken from a United States rocket launched in 1946. Taken from 65 miles (105 kilometers) above the surface, these images showed only portions of Earth, mostly desert areas in the southwestern United States.

The Blue Marble

Gradually, as technology improved, satellite photographs captured more and more of the planet. Beginning in the 1960's, spacecraft launched crews into space, giving people aboard the first view of our planet as they orbited around it. In December 1972, the crew of Apollo 17 took the most spectacular photograph of the planet ever seen. Showing the full disk of Earth, it has become known as the Blue Marble.

The name fits. The photograph shows a planet that is truly blue, covered largely by oceans. If explorers from another world saw Earth in this way for the first time, they might call it the "water planet." Indeed, dry land covers only a little more than a quarter of Earth's surface. The rest is covered by water, almost all of which is salty ocean water. Only about 3 percent of Earth's water is fresh (non-salty), and most of the fresh water is locked up in the ice of glaciers, mainly those of the polar regions.

First view from space

The Blue Marble photograph gave the first view of the South Polar Ice Cap, the vast glacier that covers the continent of Antarctica. The Mediterranean Sea is visible at the top of the photograph. The photograph shows the entire coastline of Africa, along with Madagascar, the fourth largest island in the world, off Africa's east coast. The Arabian Peninsula and the edge of the Asian mainland also stand out.

The photograph shows that the ocean is the most important feature of our planet. It ties together north and south, east and west. It surrounds and shapes the land, separates the continents, and isolates islands from one another and from the continents. In ice-covered areas near the poles, it can be difficult to see where the land ends and the sea begins. In fact, the North Polar Region—the Arctic—is more ocean than land.

Oceans, islands, and polar regions

The ocean shapes the climate and other environmental conditions of the entire Earth, but most dramatically on islands and in the polar regions. They, in turn, influence the ocean, such as when fresh water runs off from polar glaciers into the ocean.

Oceans, islands, and polar regions form **ecosystems**—interconnected webs of living things and the environment upon which they depend. When any one of these great ecosystems is affected by environmental change, either from natural causes or as a result of human activities, the others are affected as well. Pollution dumped at sea makes its way onto shorelines. Melting polar ice caps lead to rising sea waters, which may flood islands and coastal areas. Warming ocean waters create stronger hurricanes, wreaking havoc on vulnerable islands. Protecting these ecosystems begins with understanding the delicate balance that holds them together.

Oceans shape the climate of our planet most dramatically on islands, such as Fiji.

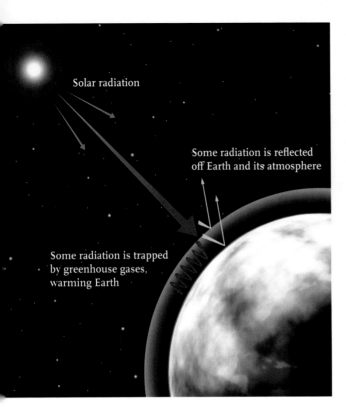

Solar radiation

Some radiation is reflected off Earth and its atmosphere

Some radiation is trapped by greenhouse gases, warming Earth

Greenhouse gases trap the sun's heat. This effect drives global warming.

A CHANGING CLIMATE

Earth's climate has always been changing. For thousands of years at a time, ice sheets covered vast regions of land. These **ice ages** were followed by thousands of years of tropical warmth, which, in turn, were followed by more ice ages. The history of the world's climate has been a cycle that gradually goes back and forth between warm periods and cool periods.

Today, many scientists warn that Earth is entering a period of **global warming.** Unlike periods of warmth in the past, scientists believe current global warming exceeds the natural cycle. Many experts predict that Earth's average temperature will rise from 2 to 11.5 °F (1.1 to 6.4 °C) by 2100. Earth's temperature has not risen so fast for hundreds of thousands, or possibly millions, of years.

The causes of global warming

Global warming is caused by an increase of certain gases in Earth's **atmosphere.** These gases trap the sun's heat much like a greenhouse, so scientists call this process the **greenhouse effect.** The gases that trap the sun's heat are called **greenhouse gases.** Most scientists agree that human activities are the main cause of a build-up of greenhouse gases in the atmosphere.

One of the main greenhouse gases is **carbon dioxide,** an invisible, odorless substance. Carbon dioxide is produced by natural sources, but many human activities, such as the burning of **fossil fuels,** give off carbon dioxide as well. Fossil fuels, which include coal, oil, and natural gas, are burned as energy to power vehicles, factories, and power plants. When fossil fuels are burned, they release carbon dioxide into the atmosphere. As more carbon dioxide collects in the atmosphere, more heat from the sun is trapped.

Green plants and other organisms absorb carbon dioxide from the air to make food. But human beings have cleared huge areas of rain forest and other places where many green plants grow. Without such plants, more carbon dioxide stays in the air.

Automobiles burn fossil fuels and release large amounts of carbon dioxide. Carbon dioxide is a greenhouse gas.

The dangers of global warming

If Earth warms up too quickly, natural ecosystems may be in danger. Plants and animals would not have enough time to **adapt** to the changing climate. Oceans would become warmer, disturbing the natural cycles of the organisms that live there. Polar environments would melt farther and faster, harming animals that have come to depend on the polar ice. And the melting polar ice caps would cause sea levels to rise, impacting islands and shorelines across the world.

Human societies, too, could be harmed by global warming. Increasing temperatures might cause global weather patterns to change, which would affect where people could grow crops. Famine (starvation caused by extreme food shortages) may hit areas that turn into desert due to the changing climate. Violent storms could become more frequent as well. Humans who live on islands and near shores could be threatened by rising sea levels. Ultimately, human beings are dependent on the natural ecosystems that global warming threatens.

What Is the Ocean?

Section Summary

The ocean is of extreme importance to Earth and its people. It contains most of Earth's water, plays a major role in the world's weather and climate, and is a source of food.

Ocean habitats are changing due to human activities, such as overfishing. Pollution from industries and general waste is also damaging ocean habitats. Scientists believe that oceans are already showing the effects of global warming, which is causing ocean temperatures to rise.

Ocean waves are caused by the movement of wind across the water.

The ocean is the vast body of salt water that covers nearly 71 percent of Earth's surface. It surrounds the continents, which separate it into five major sections: The Pacific Ocean, Atlantic Ocean, Indian Ocean, Southern Ocean, and Arctic Ocean. Together, they are known as the **world ocean.**

Seas, gulfs, and bays are parts of the oceans that extend inland or are surrounded by groups of islands. San Francisco Bay is an extension of the Pacific Ocean. The Persian Gulf is part of the Indian Ocean. The Mediterranean Sea is an arm of the Atlantic Ocean. The Sea of Japan is in the northern Pacific between the Japanese islands and the mainland of Asia. People also use the word "sea" to mean the ocean in general.

The structure of the ocean

The ocean contains 97 percent of Earth's water. Its average depth is 13,000 feet (4,000 meters), but some parts of it go down much farther. The deepest place known is the Mariana Trench, a narrow valley on the ocean floor near the island of Guam. Part of the Mariana Trench reaches down 35,840 feet (10,924 meters).

Most of the ocean lies within the great **ocean basins,** which are wide, bowl-shaped valleys between the continents. Near the coasts, shallower parts of the ocean called **continental shelves** gently slope from the edges of the continents to a depth of less than 660 feet (200 meters).

Ocean movement

The ocean is constantly in motion. The gravitational pull of the moon and sun make the tides rise and fall each day on ocean shores. Wind drives waves across the ocean's surface.

Wind also helps set great ocean currents in motion. Other forces that influence currents are water temperature and **salinity** (saltiness), the shape of the ocean bottom, and Earth's rotation. One current, the Gulf Stream, is like a huge, warm river in the ocean. Pushed by winds from the Caribbean, it flows into the Gulf of Mexico, looping around and passing Florida's coast before flowing north along the eastern coast of the United States. The Gulf Stream eventually becomes part of a great wheel of currents that flow clockwise around the North Atlantic Ocean.

The ocean's importance

The ocean plays a major role in the world's weather and climate. Most **precipitation** comes from water that **evaporates** from the ocean's surface. The ocean stores heat in summer and releases it in winter. This helps keep the world's temperature steady. Warm currents, such as the Gulf Stream, can make winter temperatures along coasts warmer than inland areas.

The ocean's role in climate is not the only way it affects people. Human beings have used the ocean surface as a highway for thousands of years. Fish and other ocean products are critical food sources. The ocean can also provide drinking water after its salt is removed.

In addition, the ocean is home to a large number of complex, beautiful **ecosystems.** Colorful coral reefs and underwater **kelp** forests provide shelter for huge numbers of organisms. Scientists have only begun to explore the bizarre world of the deep ocean.

Together, the oceans and seas form the world ocean, which covers nearly 71 percent of Earth's surface.

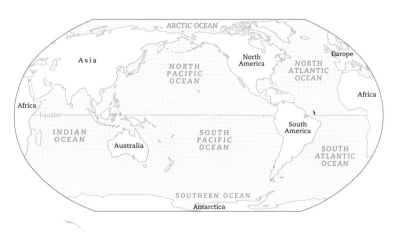

Tiny zooplankton called krill are the main diet of Earth's largest animal, the blue whale.

THE SURFACE

Life in the ocean exists mostly in the sunlit area within 330 feet (100 meters) of the water's surface. This area is called the **photic** (*FOH tihk*) **zone.** Below it, not enough sunlight penetrates for plants and other organisms to carry out **photosynthesis** (*FOH tuh SIHN thuh sihs*), the process by which they use sunlight to make food.

Ocean pastures

The part of the photic zone richest in life lies over the continental shelves. Waters there are full of nutrients (nourishing substances) washed off nearby land. Many tiny organisms thrive in such areas, drifting in the surface waters. These organisms are collectively called **plankton.**

Plankton is made up of two kinds of organisms. The first kind, called **phytoplankton,** are plantlike organisms that use photosynthesis to make food. Many of them have only one cell. Among the most numerous phytoplankton are a type of single-celled alga called **diatoms.** The cells of diatoms are enclosed in a hard, glasslike shell. Another kind of phytoplankton, called dinoflagellates (*DIH nuh FLAJ uh layts*), propel themselves through the water with two tail-like structures.

The rest of the plankton is called **zooplankton.** The zooplankton are tiny animals and animallike organisms that eat the phytoplankton. Some zooplankton eat one another as well. Small worms, newly hatched fish, single-celled organisms, and other young organisms make up the zooplankton.

Surface giants

The biggest creatures in the sea depend on the tiniest for food. Shrimplike zooplankton called **krill** are the main diet of Earth's largest animal, the blue whale. Blue whales are mammals (warm-blooded animals that feed their young with mother's milk) that grow up to 100 feet (30 meters) long. The largest fish, the 40-foot (12-meter) whale shark, also feeds on zooplankton, though it also feeds on small fish. Whale sharks use special filters in their gills to strain zooplankton from the water.

Plankton provide food for fish both large and small, such as this blue shark off the coast of California.

The plankton also serves as a food source for many small fish. Schools of tiny fish, including menhaden and sardines, regularly roam the surface feeding on plankton. These small fish, in turn, are eaten by larger fish, such as bluefish and tuna. Many species (kinds) of sharks, including the great white shark, also cruise near the surface in search of prey, such as seals and sea lions.

Although some seals and sea lions can dive to great depths, most feed in surface waters. So do penguins, which depend on small fish as a food source. A vast number of sea birds patrol the skies over the sea's surface in search of fish and other creatures to eat. Some of these sea birds, such as albatrosses, are loners. Others, such as gulls and terns, tend to feed in flocks. The sight and sound of a few terns diving into the water can quickly bring dozens, even hundreds, of others to the area in search of a meal.

Countershading

Many fish found in surface waters have developed a form of **camouflage** (*KAM uh flahzh*) to protect them from enemies both above and below. They have dark backs and light bellies. From above, they blend into the darker color of the water. From below, they blend into the sunlight. This form of coloration is called **countershading.**

In an environment lit from above, countershading gives fish the appearance of even shading. Such shading makes it more difficult for predators to gain a sense of the animals' depth, complicating attacks. Some deep water fish have special organs that produce light on the bottom of their bodies. This special kind of countershading obscures a fish's silhouette from below.

This white tip shark is camouflaged with countershading.

What Is the Ocean?   11

CORAL REEFS

Some of the most diverse plant and animal life in the ocean can be found in rocklike formations called coral reefs. The reefs consist of a **limestone** structure that is made by a group of jellyfishlike animals called **polyps.** The coral itself consists of colonies of these tiny animals, which build the coral reef by depositing small amounts of limestone around their lower bodies. They create the limestone from chemicals that occur naturally in seawater. As new polyps grow, so does the build-up of limestone.

Coral consists of tiny animals called polyps. These mushroom soft coral polyps live in the Pacific Ocean.

Coral reefs are confined to the shallow ocean waters of the tropics and subtropics because the polyps need warm water. Corals also need plenty of sunlight, so most reefs are no deeper than 100 feet (30 meters), and none grow below the photic zone. Polyps also cannot make reefs in water darkened by pollution.

A world of reefs

Reefs are a large part of the ocean world, covering about 116,000 square miles (300,000 square kilometers). Some reefs are immense. The Great Barrier Reef off northern Australia is more than 1,240 miles (2,000 kilometers) long.

Only the outer surface of the reef contains living polyps. Underneath are layers of coral built by millions upon millions of polyps in the past and left behind when they die. Cemented into the coral are the shells and other remains of sea animals that once lived in the reef. These materials help build its size.

Ocean apartment houses

Coral reefs have the most diverse life of any ocean **habitat**, acting like multi-storied apartment houses for plants and animals. The surface of the reef is covered with what appear to be large, colorful plants. However, these organisms are really animals, such as sponges or coral polyps that grow in the shape of antlers or bushes. Other corals, which do not produce limestone, are shaped like feathers or fans. Sea anemones—which are animals but resemble flowers—wave their tentacles to catch drifting plankton. Barnacles are also found here, permanently glued to the surface of reefs.

Coral reefs are filled with holes, cracks, crevices, and caves that provide shelter for many sea animals. Bright red squirrelfish hide in caves that tunnel through the reef. Spiny lobsters take shelter in the reef's narrow cracks. Many kinds of algae live on, and in, the coral.

The reefs are also filled with hunting predators. Moray eels, with jaws full of needlelike teeth, snake through the reefs hunting octopus and crabs. Small fish called wrasses search the reefs for shrimp and other prey. Colorful parrotfish crunch coral in beaklike jaws to feed on algae and the polyps themselves. Sea turtles, barracuda, and groupers swim around the reef. Many species of shark live on reefs, and some of them form hunting groups that search the reefs for prey. Reef fish also include grunts, snappers, tangs, and butterfly fish.

Coral reefs provide homes for a stunning diversity of ocean life.

UNDERWATER FORESTS

Large beds of huge brown seaweed called **kelp** grow in cool waters along rocky coasts in several parts of the ocean. Swaying in the currents and waves like trees in the wind, kelp beds are commonly known as kelp forests.

Some kelp forests cover hundreds of square miles. The larger forests grow where water temperatures are between 50 and 65 °F (10 and 18 °C), while smaller forests are generally found in warmer waters. In 2007, a kelp forest was found in the tropical Pacific near the Galapagos Islands.

These giant kelp off the coast of California can grow up to 1 foot (0.3 meters) per day.

Giant algae

Although kelp gets its food from sunlight, kelp is not a plant. Like most other seaweed, kelp is actually a kind of alga. There are many different types of kelp. One of the biggest is the giant kelp. Growing at a rate of up to 1 foot (0.3 meters) per day, giant kelp can reach a length of 200 feet (60 meters). Immense giant kelp forests grow off the Pacific coast of North America, especially California.

As an alga, giant kelp lacks the true roots, stems, and leaves that plants have. But giant kelp resembles a tree in some ways. A root-like structure called a holdfast anchors the giant kelp to a rocky surface. A frond, which resembles a stem and leaf, extends from the holdfast. A giant kelp's fronds have air-filled, balloonlike structures called bladders attached to them. The bladders cause the fronds to float up toward the surface, where they can better absorb sunlight for photosynthesis.

Kelp forest creatures

Like forests on land, kelp forests are home to a large number of animals. About 800 animal species have been recorded living in California's kelp forests. They include such **invertebrates** as starfish, octopuses, sea anemones, sea worms, crabs, and sea slugs. Fish come to kelp forests for shelter and food. Leopard sharks, opaleye, snapper, trumpeter sea dragons, and cowfish swim between the kelp.

Mammals live in and around kelp forests as well. Sea lions

chase fish beneath the canopy of fronds. Harbor seals pop their heads up through the kelp for a look around for food. Sea otters float belly-up in the kelp, resting or eating prey brought up from below.

Sea otters are especially important to the health of kelp forests because they eat spiny invertebrates called sea urchins. A sea urchin's favorite food is kelp. If the number of sea urchins in a kelp forest grows too large, the urchins eat all the kelp and destroy the forest. Sea otters help keep sea urchins under control.

Sea otters live off the coasts of the northern Pacific from Japan to California. In the past, they were hunted almost to extinction for their fur. They have recovered but are still endangered. Oil spills and other forms of pollution threaten them. Their numbers remain low in many areas.

Without sea otters to feed on sea urchins, kelp forests may be in danger.

Many invertebrates, such as the giant sunflower sea star, live in kelp forests.

A CLOSER LOOK
Uses of Kelp

People have many uses for giant kelp. It contains the salt potassium chloride, which is used to make fertilizer and gunpowder. It also contains iodine, which is an essential nutrient. Kelp's most important product is a chemical called algin (*AL jihn*), a gummy material found in the cell walls of the kelp.

Algin is important to many industries. It is used in some medical dressings and to make molds that produce dental appliances and artificial limbs. The food industry uses it to thicken soups and jellies, and to give ice cream a creamy texture.

In many countries, kelp is collected from areas where it grows naturally. People in China and Japan grow kelp on special farms in the ocean.

Sea turtles cross the open ocean to reach beaches where they breed.

OCEAN DESERTS

The open ocean lacks the great variety of habitats that are available on reefs, in kelp forests, or near shores. In every direction, the environment of the open ocean is the same: A blue expanse of rolling waves, mile after countless mile. The bottom is too far down to provide shelter. The shore is too far away to provide nutrients, causing phytoplankton to be scarce. As a result, zooplankton—which feed on phytoplankton—are also scarce, as are all the other creatures further along the **food chain.** Living things are few and far between. Compared to inshore waters, the open ocean is like a desert.

As with deserts on land, some animals do live in the open ocean. Many of them have to be big, strong, and fast enough to travel long distances. These creatures include certain whales, sea turtles, marlin, and sharks.

Long-distance travelers

Many animals migrate across the open ocean. They travel thousands of miles to and from regions closer to shores, where they feed and give birth.

Sea turtles regularly travel across the open ocean to reach beaches where they breed each year. One group of green sea turtles nests on Ascension Island in the South Atlantic. The turtles feed off the coast of Brazil, more than 1,300 miles (2,092 kilometers) across the open sea.

Humpback whales migrate
across thousands of miles
of open ocean every year.

Humpback whales migrate up to 5,000 miles (8,000 kilometers) each way. Humpbacks spend most of the year in shallow coastal waters.

One group of humpbacks winters off the Hawaiian Islands. There, they mate and give birth. During this period, they do not feed, instead living on fat stored up from summer. In spring, the whales leave Hawaii and head for waters off Alaska. There, they eat up to a ton of krill and small fish each day. Cold waters, like those in the northern Pacific, have more nutrients and support more plankton than warm tropical waters, like those off Hawaii.

Some large fish travel equally long distances, or even longer. In 2005, scientists reported tracking a great white shark on a vast journey. This shark, which the scientists named Nicole, swam from South Africa to Australia and then back again. The total distance covered was more than 12,000 miles (20,000 kilometers). The shark was tagged with a transmitter and then tracked by satellite. It took 99 days for it to travel to Australia. Six months later, the shark was spotted in waters near South Africa. Scientists now believe that great whites near Australia and Africa may have contact with one another.

The American eel lives most of its life in rivers, lakes, and bays along the Atlantic coast of the United States and Canada. The European eel has a similar home along the Atlantic coast of Europe. After reaching adulthood, the eels from both sides of the Atlantic travel across the open ocean to the Sargasso Sea, between the West Indies and Azores islands. Although the sea is in the center of the ocean, an odd seaweed called sargassum is **adapted** to grow there. A combination of wind and currents trap the seaweed in this part of the ocean. Once they reach the Sargasso Sea, the eels reproduce. The tiny young are carried by currents, such as the Gulf Stream, back to the continents.

Sargassum seaweed

THE OCEAN BOTTOM

The deep ocean is a world of pitch-black darkness. Most of the sun's rays can penetrate only as far as about 130 feet (40 meters) below the surface, with the last traces of light disappearing at about 650 feet (200 meters). The pressure of the water in the deep is so great that it would crush the human body. The water in the deep also reaches near-freezing temperatures.

High mountains, deep canyons

If all water were drained from the ocean, the ocean bottom might look astonishing, but not unfamiliar. The ocean bottom has some of the same features as land—mountains, ridges, plains, valleys, and canyons.

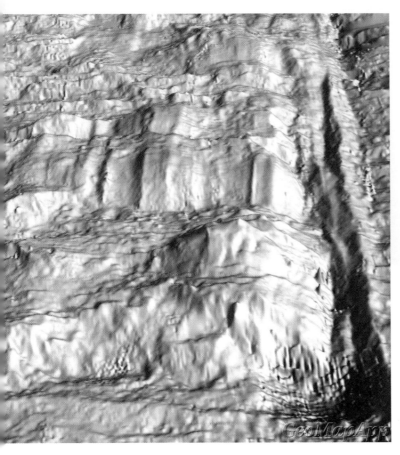

The Mid-Atlantic Ridge, part of which is shown above as a computerized image, includes mountain chains, deep canyons, and valleys.

A chain of mountains runs through the entire ocean. Scientists estimate it is from 30,000 to 50,000 miles (50,000 to 80,000 kilometers) long. The sections of the mountain chain in the middle of each ocean basin have their own names, such as the Mid-Atlantic Ridge and the East Pacific Rise. Most of the mountains in the ridges rise about 5,000 feet (1,500 meters) above the sea floor. Deep canyons and valleys cut through the ridges. Other canyons cut into the vast, flat **abyssal plains** that stretch across the ocean bottom from ridge to ridge.

Creatures of the deep

The deep ocean is home to some of the most bizarre creatures on Earth. They include bulbous octopuses, huge worms, and glass-like sponges that look like delicate flowers.

Without light, phytoplankton cannot grow in the deep. The food chain is mostly based on falling bits and pieces of dead organisms from above, called **marine snow.** Some animals of the depths, such as sponges, filter tiny bits of marine snow through

their bodies for food. Others, such as crabs and many types of worms, feast on large, dead animals that fall to the depths. Still other deep-sea animals eat these scavengers, and each other.

This Colobonema jellyfish produces light to confuse predators.

The bodies of deep-sea animals are very watery, almost jelly-like, so they can resist the great pressure. Squeezing them would be like pushing down on a plastic bag full of water. Many deep-sea animals produce their own form of light. In the endless darkness, their living light helps them recognize members of the same species, attract prey, and confuse predators. Deep-sea angler fish have a tab of light atop their snout that acts like a lure to attract smaller fish.

Although most fishes of the deep ocean are small, many have monstrous features. The swallower fish, for example, has huge jaws that reach back to the rear of its head. It can gulp down prey of its own size, which it digests in a belly that swells like a balloon.

A CLOSER LOOK

Ocean Hot Springs

In 1977, scientists discovered a hot spring on the floor of the Pacific Ocean near the coast of Ecuador. Many others have been discovered since then. These springs, called **hydrothermal vents,** lie along the undersea ridges that form part of the great undersea mountain chain. They form where magma (molten rock) seeps through Earth's crust on the ocean bottom. The water that spouts from these vents is very hot, with temperatures as high as 840 °F (450 °C). Large numbers of organisms live near the vents, including giant tube worms up to 8 feet (2.4 meters) long. The worms live on bacteria that make food from the chemicals released by the hydrothermal vents.

Hydrothermal vent

OVERFISHING

You may have heard the saying, "There are plenty of fish in the sea." This saying is no longer true. The numbers of ocean fish—especially fish that people eat—have dramatically declined. Pollution and development have contributed to their decrease, and climate change may also play a role. However, the main reason that many formerly common fish are vanishing is overfishing. Fishing fleets simply have taken too many fish out of the ocean.

When people take large numbers of fish from the ocean, its ecological balance can become disrupted.

Vanishing fisheries

Fish is an important part of people's diet around the world, especially in less developed countries. Many people in Asia, for example, get much of their protein from fish, and most fish come from the ocean. However, the supply of fish is not endless, and many fish stocks in the ocean are threatened.

For centuries, the waters off eastern Canada and New England supported a major fishery for such ocean fish as Atlantic cod, halibut, and flounder. Today, the fish populations are almost gone. The United States and Canada have closed off some areas and severely limited the number of fish that can be caught in others. Limits have even been placed on the number of days individual fishing boats can be on the fishing grounds.

With catches dropping, fleets have turned to species that have not traditionally been fished **commercially.** These include monkfish and the Patagonian toothfish, also called the Chilean sea bass. These fish, too, are increasingly in danger.

Overfishing affects more than just the species that are sought. As the overfished species dwindles, so do the fish that prey on that species. Thus, the ecological balance of the ocean is disrupted.

Causes of overfishing

The basic cause of overfishing is that many countries and the fishing industry have shown little concern for **conserving** fish.

Fishing nets often contain bycatch.

Fish Farms

Fish farms are a possible solution to overfishing if they are operated properly. The most successful fish farms have involved such freshwater fish as catfish and rainbow trout. These fish eat inexpensive food and can be kept in artificial ponds. Even if the pond water becomes polluted, it can be controlled and prevented from entering natural waterways.

Another kind of fish farming—involving nets set up in the ocean—is more problematic. Salmon raised in this way have escaped and spread disease and parasites, such as fish lice, to wild fish. Such farms can also produce large concentrations of liquid waste.

Only recently have some countries begun to scientifically manage fisheries in their waters to keep fish populations at proper levels. There are few international agreements covering fishing on the high seas.

During the last half-century, fishing boats have become larger, faster, and more efficient. They let out nets and long lines that stretch for miles, carrying thousands of hooks. This type of gear catches not only edible fish, but also many others, which often die and are discarded as **bycatch.** Whales, dolphins, sea turtles, and even sea birds perish as bycatch in fishing nets. Nets abandoned at sea may continue to catch victims for years. Some nets hauled behind boats across the bottom are so big that they smash reefs and destroy the habitats of bottom-dwelling creatures.

Conserving fish

Some scientists are pushing for nations and the fishing industry to adopt conservation practices. For example, certain fish species could be put off limits for fishing until their numbers recover, and countries could establish protected areas in which the fish can recover. Fisheries could design equipment that targets only specific fish to reduce bycatch.

Conservation has worked in the past. In the 1980's, striped bass were vanishing along the East Coast of the United States. Then severe limits were placed upon fishing for striped bass. Today, the bass have recovered and are abundant.

Salmon farm in Norway

What Is the Ocean?   21

OCEAN POLLUTION

Ocean pollution takes many forms, from small plastic bags tossed into the water to huge tanker ships spilling millions of gallons of oil. An oil spill can threaten the life of entire coastlines, but even a plastic bag can be harmful. A sea turtle, for instance, might eat the bag, mistaking it for a jellyfish, and choke.

Oil spills

The world uses about 83.6 million barrels of oil a day. Some oil is transported over land by pipelines and trucks, but most is moved over water in barges and enormous ocean-going ships called tankers.

Oil spills, such as this spill from the *Exxon Valdez*, can threaten the life of entire coastlines.

Oil is stored in huge tanks and processed into gasoline and other products at **refineries.** Oil can spill or leak from any of these sources. Spills are caused by human error, equipment breakdown, storms or earthquakes, and by such criminal acts as illegal dumping, vandalism, or terrorism.

Oil is a particularly harmful type of ocean pollution because it floats on water and spreads rapidly. Even when thinly distributed, oil is extremely dangerous to ocean life. It coats the bodies of sea birds so they cannot fly. When the birds try to clean themselves, they are poisoned. Oil also poisons fish and smothers shellfish and other animals on the ocean floor.

Pollution from land

Much ocean pollution drains into the sea from the land. **Pollutants** include poisonous chemicals and **fertilizers** from farms, **sewage,** and **by-products** of modern industry. These pollutants enter rivers or storm drains, and eventually flow into the ocean.

Fertilizers can cause large amounts of algae to grow on the surface of water, creating **algal blooms.** When the algae die, bacteria use oxygen from the water to break down the algae. Without oxygen, the water turns into a lifeless **dead zone.** One such dead zone in the Gulf of Mexico covers about 11,000 square miles (18,000 square kilometers). It is caused by algal blooms that feed on fertilizer runoff that drains from farms into the Mississippi

River, which flows into the Gulf of Mexico.

Ocean pollution has increased partly because people have developed large areas of coastline. Housing, industry, and resorts now crowd ocean shores. According to a **United Nations** report, nearly half the world's population lives within 93 miles (150 kilometers) of the coast. Eighty percent of the world's tourism is also concentrated there. Such coastal developments dump pollution into the ocean, and they can also destroy seashore ecosystems.

Algal blooms such as this one in the Philippines can cause dead zones that stretch for thousands of square miles.

Fighting pollution

Scientists, governments, and industries are seeking ways to allow development along the ocean while reducing pollution. One way may be to reduce dependence on oil. Scientists have begun developing **biofuels** from plant material as an alternate source of energy. However, some scientists argue that the plants used to make biofuels, such as corn, require lots of energy to grow. Therefore, biofuel production is responsible for large amounts of **carbon dioxide emissions.** Biofuel plants may also be grown with fertilizers, which pollute waterways and can cause algal blooms.

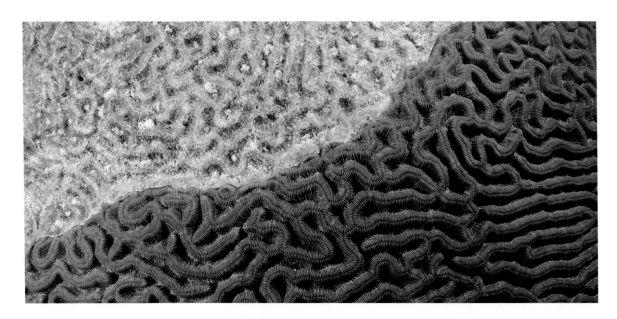

Coral bleaching can occur when algae are expelled from coral polyps due to warming ocean waters.

CLIMATE CHANGE AND THE OCEAN

Some scientists believe **global warming** is already harming ocean life. If global temperatures continue to increase, scientists worry that ocean ecosystems will change drastically, with many of the ocean's living things unable to adapt.

Colorless corals

Warming ocean waters near coral reefs can lead to **coral bleaching**, a process where corals lose their brilliant colors and become white. Healthy corals get their colors from tiny algae that live inside their bodies. But when the water temperature rises, the algae are expelled from the coral polyps, and the reefs may die.

A number of factors can cause coral bleaching, so scientists are not certain that global warming is behind every observed case. However, if the ocean temperature warms significantly from increased global warming, more reefs will be in danger.

Carbon dioxide and the ocean

Global warming is caused in part by an excess of **carbon dioxide** gas, but not all carbon dioxide goes into the **atmosphere.** While forests absorb much of this carbon dioxide, the ocean absorbs about one-third of it. As the ocean absorbs more carbon dioxide, its water chemistry may change, becoming more acidic. Acidic water can eat away at the shells of many ocean-dwelling creatures, such as shellfish and tiny diatoms. If these creatures are harmed, the entire food chain could be affected.

Warming and currents

Some scientists warn that global warming could severely change the flow of ocean currents. Ocean currents circulate water from one end of the world ocean to the other. They also contribute to a vertical mixing of ocean water. Cold, heavy water from the poles sinks as the currents push it toward the equator, and then flows back up to the surface as it warms near the tropics. This endless mixing of the ocean water helps control Earth's climate.

Scientists fear that global warming could disturb the flow of currents, which would cause even greater climate changes across Earth. For example, as more freshwater glaciers melt in the Arctic from global warming, the salinity (salt content) of the water decreases. Water with lower salinity sinks more slowly than water with a high salt content. Scientists are not sure to what extent this could affect the ocean currents.

The circulation of ocean water prevents northern regions from getting too cold and tropical regions from getting too hot.

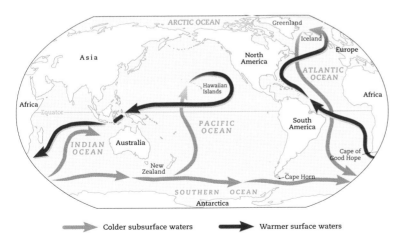

A CLOSER LOOK
The Food Chain

Organisms that live in the ocean depend on a highly complex food chain that starts with phytoplankton, which create food from the sun's energy. Phytoplankton are eaten by zooplankton, which are in turn eaten by other zooplankton and small fish. The small fish provide food for larger fish, and so on.

Global warming can disturb the ocean food chain. Diatoms (a type of phytoplankton) may be threatened by more acidic ocean water from excessive carbon dioxide. Fewer diatoms would mean fewer zooplankton, such as krill. Reduced numbers of krill could mean fewer fish and whales. A decrease in diatoms could disrupt the entire ocean food chain.

Microscopic view of diatom shells

What Are Islands?

Section Summary

Islands are home to many plant and animal species not found on continents. These unique ecosystems are being disrupted by human activities, such as pollution from industries and introduced plants and animals not native to islands.

Climate change is a serious threat to islands. Global warming may cause sea levels to rise, flooding many islands. It may also cause stronger storms, such as hurricanes, which can severely damage island habitats.

Islands can be found in oceans, rivers, and lakes throughout the world.

An island is a land mass smaller than a continent that is surrounded by water. New, small islands form and disappear all the time. The largest island, Greenland, is nearly the size of a continent.

Scientists group islands into five classes, according to the way in which they formed. They are (1) continental islands, (2) tectonically formed islands, (3) volcanic islands, (4) coral islands, and (5) barrier islands.

Continental islands

Continental islands are islands that were once attached to a continent. For example, the small islands that dot the bays and inlets off the shores of the northeastern United States were once hilltops and ridges overlooking coastal valleys. When the last **ice age** glaciers melted about 11,000 years ago, the sea flooded the valleys and surrounded the uplands, which became islands. On a far larger scale, this is how the islands of Great Britain were separated from the European continent. A vast glacier that once stretched from the Arctic to the Thames River melted, leaving the North Sea in its place. Other continental islands form when streams and ocean waves wear away the land between an area of coastline, such as a peninsula, and the rest of the mainland.

Tectonically formed islands

Tectonically formed islands are created by slow movements of immense pieces of Earth's crust called **tectonic plates.** The continents ride upon these plates. About 200 million years ago, plate movement split the continents apart from a single, massive "supercontinent." Smaller pieces of detached land became large islands, such as Greenland and Madagascar.

Moving very slowly, the plates shove and grind against one another. When the edge of one plate rides over another, pieces from the bottom may scrape off and pile up to form other tectonic islands, such as Barbados in the West Indies and Kodiak Island off Alaska.

Volcanic islands

Plate movement helps trigger volcanic eruptions, which cause lava and ash from under the sea to pile up. When such piles break the surface of the ocean, they form islands, such as the Hawaiian Islands. Long, curving chains of volcanic islands that rise along the edges of trenches in the ocean floor are called island arcs. The Aleutian Islands and the islands of Japan are examples of island arcs.

Coral islands

Coral reefs can build up until they become islands. Sometimes coral islands form around volcanic islands that sink. The circle of coral that remains behind is called an **atoll.** Coral can be among the materials that build up around the roots of mangroves, which are tropical trees that can grow in shallow ocean areas. The build-up around a cluster of mangroves can create exposed land, on which other plants and animals can live.

Barrier islands

Barrier islands are made of sand, **silt,** and gravel distributed by waves in lines of dunes parallel to the coast. These "barriers" are separated from the mainland by sheltered bays and lagoons. They protect the mainland from storms and waves. However, storms sometimes wash away barriers. Long stretches of barrier islands edge the east coast of the United States south of New England.

In 1963, Surtsey, a new volcanic island, appeared near the coast of Iceland.

ISLAND PLANTS

The longer an island has been cut off from other land and the farther away it lies, the more its life differs from plants and animals elsewhere. Over time, island life evolves (gradually develops) into unique species not found on continents. Many species live on certain groups of islands or even just a single island.

The silverswords

On the islands of Hawaii and Maui, there are three species of plants called silverswords. Their name comes from their sword-shaped leaves, which are covered

Silverswords live only on the Hawaiian Islands.

with fine, silvery hairs. The flowering part of the plant can stand taller than an adult man.

Silverswords live only on Hawaii and Maui, and each species grows only in particular areas. One species grows at certain elevation ranges on Hawaii's Mauna Kea and Mauna Loa volcanoes. Another species grows on the slopes of the Haleakala volcano, in Maui, and a third species grows on top of Mount Eke and Puu Kukui, also in Maui.

The silverswords are examples of the many rare island plants that grow only in a particular **habitat**, sometimes only in a single place. Such species usually cannot survive in places other than where they evolved. They are **adapted** only to the environment in which they are found.

How plants get to islands

Islands that are far from the continents often have fewer plant species than islands closer to the mainland. Some plants reach islands directly from the continents, while others travel from island to island across the ocean.

Plants travel across the ocean in several ways. Some seeds float to islands, drifting on currents and waves. The coconut palm, for instance, may have originated in South America or southern Asia. The tree may have originally spread to islands when co-

Whitebeam trees in the United Kingdom are distinct from whitebeams in the rest of Europe.

conuts—which contain the plant's seeds—fell into the sea.

Winds also blow seeds to islands. The air in the middle of the ocean may contain seeds, spores, and even insects carried in the breeze. Seeds can also reach islands when birds that have eaten the seeds carry them to the island through their droppings.

Plants can reach new islands surprisingly fast. The volcanic island of Surtsey first appeared out of the ocean near Iceland in 1963. By 1965, complex plants were already beginning to grow on the beach. As new soil forms on new islands, more and more plants can grow there.

Plants already on islands

Islands that were once part of continents often have plant life similar to the land from which they split. Eventually, however, new types of plants, different from those on the mainland, may develop. The United Kingdom, for example, has a few kinds of whitebeam tree that are closely related to, but still different from, whitebeams on the main European continent.

Some islands are particularly famous for the large number of species that grow only there. For example, of the more than 600 species of ferns that grow on Mount Kinabalu in Borneo, 50 species are found nowhere else. And of the 10 species of pitcher plants there, 4 are found nowhere else.

Borneo is home to a variety of plant life, such as this pitcher plant.

ISLAND ANIMALS

Many animals reach islands in the same ways plants do. Small creatures, such as insects and baby spiders, are carried by the winds. Some animals float to islands, either by themselves or by hitching a ride on driftwood and other plant material.

Other animals can reach even distant islands by swimming. Saltwater crocodiles, which inhabit many islands in southern Asia and the South Pacific, can travel hundreds of miles across the sea. Birds and bats can fly to islands. Bats inhabit some islands where few other mammals exist.

In Hawaii, a variety of birds, such as the 'I'iwi, evolved from a single species that arrived millions of years ago.

How islands change animals

Like plants, island animals often evolve into new forms not found elsewhere. Many cannot survive away from their island homes. Islands that are far from other land have no life at first, but may end up with a unique variety of animals.

Between three and five million years ago, a species of bird that probably belonged to the finch family landed on the Hawaiian Islands. These birds most likely came from North America. Hardly any predators existed on the islands, and few other birds had reached them.

The newly arrived birds spread quickly through forests that still had little other bird life. Scientists believe that they ate seeds by crushing them with their short, cone-shaped bills, much the way finches do today. Eventually, however, some of them developed long, curved bills adapted to feeding on nectar in tube-shaped flowers. These birds, called Hawaiian honeycreepers, later developed bills of several other shapes, adapted to feeding on different foods. Some, for instance, had short, straight bills for prying insects out of tree bark. The appearance of the honeycreepers changed, too. Their colors ranged from drab olive green

to bright crimson. What started as one species had become several dozen.

Island refuges

Islands can provide refuges for species that once were widespread but have vanished elsewhere. Madagascar is the home of primitive primates called lemurs. They or their ancestors probably arrived there from Africa on floating vegetation. Lemurs disappeared from Africa millions of years ago. They could not compete with the continent's better-adapted primates, the monkeys and apes. However, monkeys and apes never reached Madagascar, so lemurs survive there.

Change is slow

Madagascar began to break away from Africa sometime between 50 and 80 million years ago, so the island has had plenty of time to develop unique life. Great Britain, on the other hand, was connected to the European continent until recently—only about 8,500 years ago, after melting glacier ice flooded the English Channel. Not enough time has passed for the wildlife of Great Britain to change much from that of nearby areas of Europe.

Great Britain shares some animal life with the European continent, including red deer, roe deer, red foxes, badgers, otters, and the European hare. But while dozens of species of snakes inhabit Europe, Great Britain has only a few.

Lemurs survive on the island of Madagascar, but they have disappeared from the rest of Africa.

Invasive species can wreak havoc on native species. This tree frog, called the coqui, has invaded the Hawaiian Islands.

INVASIVE SPECIES

A species that is loved on one island can be a pest, even a threat, on another. An example is the coqui, a tree frog native to Puerto Rico that has been transplanted to Hawaii. Puerto Ricans consider it a national emblem, but the government of Hawaii is trying to exterminate it. The coqui—named for the *ko-kee* sound of the male's call—is an **invasive species** in Hawaii. An invasive species is a plant or animal that has been introduced and established in a place other than its native home and threatens the ecological balance there. Some invasive species also threaten people and their livelihoods.

Invasion routes

Islands are especially vulnerable to invasive species. Because many islands are isolated and have so many unique plants and animals, introducing a new species can threaten an island's fragile ecological balance. A newly introduced species often has no natural predators on an island to keep its population under control. Some invasive species can better compete for food and resources with native animals, while others eat native animals.

Invasive species can be brought on purpose, such as the pigs, monkeys, dogs, and other animals that European sailors took to the Indian Ocean island of Mauritius in the 1600's. The animals helped kill off the last of the now-extinct dodo birds. Often, invasive species arrive by accident, in cargo carried by airplanes or ships. Coquis probably reached Hawaii in a shipment of plants from Puerto Rico.

Hawaii's coqui problem

Coquis first appeared in Hawaii during the 1990's and quickly multiplied out of control. In Puerto Rico, such predators as snakes control coqui numbers. Other frogs compete with them for food. Hawaii, however, has no native snakes or amphibians, so coquis have free rein there.

The noise from coquis is so bothersome that it is difficult to sell homes where large numbers of coquis live. Hotels are worried the noise will drive away tourists.

Coquis also threaten Hawaii's bird populations. They feed on insects and other **invertebrates** that Hawaii's few surviving forest birds need for food. As the number of coquis increases, the birds' food supply diminishes.

Vanishing Hawaiian birds

The story of Hawaii's birds is one of the most dramatic examples of how islands can suffer from invasive species. Hawaii once had about 70 species of native birds. Since humans arrived there, 28 species have vanished. Almost all the survivors are endangered. Introduced cats, dogs, goats, pigs, rabbits, and rats killed off the native birds. Introduced livestock destroyed plants that served as shelter and food for the birds. More than three-quarters of Hawaii's native forests have been cleared for agriculture.

Between 1826 and 1830, the southern house mosquito came to Hawaii in ships from North and South America. It spread avian malaria, a disease that killed many birds. To make matters worse, pigs that escaped from farms chewed holes in the trunks of Hawaiian tree ferns. Rain collected in these holes, providing excellent breeding pools for the mosquitoes.

Methods of control

In order to keep out invasive species, some countries prohibit the importation of certain species or materials in which they can travel, such as untreated wooden packing material.

Controlling invasive species once they arrive can be difficult. Current methods include trapping them or uprooting plants in which they live, spraying poisonous chemicals, or introducing a natural enemy to their environment. The Hawaiian government has sprayed the chemical citric acid in an attempt to reduce coqui populations.

A CLOSER LOOK
The Brown Tree Snake

The brown tree snake is an invasive species that has caused much damage to the island of Guam in the western Pacific Ocean. Native to eastern Australia, New Guinea, and the Solomon Islands, the brown tree snake arrived on Guam with cargo during World War II. With no predators to control its numbers, the snake has helped eliminate 9 of the 22 native bird species and 4 of the 10 native lizards.

The brown tree snake's bite is poisonous, and it sometimes attacks infants or small children. The snake also climbs electric power lines and causes short circuits and power outages, inflicting millions of dollars in damage.

The brown tree snake

Laysan albatrosses bring plastic and other floating trash to the remote island of Midway.

ISLAND POLLUTION

Islands are threatened by pollution both on land and at sea. Pollution can become concentrated on small and isolated islands. Some islands, for instance, have only a few sources of fresh water, which can easily become polluted. When islanders develop such industries as mining or logging, runoff and pollution from these activities can threaten the entire island.

Pollution from the sea

Almost every form of ocean pollution finds its way to islands. Oil from ships often pollutes island shores. This oil is not necessarily from accidental spills. Ships sometimes illegally discharge oil and other wastes at sea.

Pollution of many kinds, such as **pesticides** and industrial waste, reaches islands from the ocean. Some of them come from sources far away. In the 1990's, scientists on the small, remote island of Midway in the Pacific Ocean found that some **pollutants** had originated as far as 2,000 miles (3,219 kilometers) away. They also found plastic and other trash on the island from sources beyond its shores. Some of the trash was brought to Midway by Laysan albatrosses, large sea birds that nest there. The birds may have mistaken the trash for food and brought it to the island to feed their young. Floating plastic cigarette lighters were among the most common items found.

Pollution from land

The human population on islands tends to be concentrated near the shores. A high concentration of people can create pollution from **sewage**, solid waste, pesticides, and **fertilizers.** Tourism can benefit islands economically, especially in less developed parts of the world. But facilities for tourists also tend to cluster near the coast, increasing the concentration of pollutants.

Development, such as mining and forestry in island interiors, can help improve an island's economy. However, such development must be carefully **regulated** (controlled) so it does not cause environmental damage. Uncontrolled logging, for instance, can leave hillsides bare and vulnerable to **erosion**, which washes away the soil.

Erosion can cause water sources to become polluted when fine grains of soil, rock, or other materials wash into water supplies. In addition, eroded soil can prevent **ground water** (water stored underground) supplies from being replenished by rain. Instead of soaking into the soil, the rainwater quickly washes across the eroded land into the ocean.

The **United Nations** Convention on Biodiversity, signed in 1992 by 157 nations, warns that pollution from liquid and solid waste harms wildlife on land and at sea. Solid waste, such as plastics, cardboard, and metal, piles up in garbage dumps that are often placed too close to natural habitats. The tropical region—where many islands are located—is especially vulnerable to the loss of natural habitats. Scientists believe that more than 10 times as many species live in the tropics as the Arctic.

Air pollution is a problem on certain islands, just as it is a problem in large mainland cities. Forest fires in Indonesia pollute the air over the islands of Singapore. Air pollution from industry and vehicles has been increasing even on islands far out in the Indian Ocean and on the sunny islands of the Bahamas.

GREEN FACT

Erosion occurs when the land is stripped bare, often by such industrial activity as mining and logging. Water quickly washes over eroded land, which can spread pollutants and harm water supplies on islands.

Uncontrolled logging on islands can cause rapid erosion, washing away soil and spreading pollutants.

CLIMATE CHANGE AND ISLANDS

Scientists believe that **global warming** will cause at least part of the polar ice caps to melt. This, in turn, will cause the sea level to rise. According to some climate computer models, sea levels could rise several feet or meters if ice sheets on Antarctica and Greenland melt into the ocean.

Sea-level rise is of special concern to island inhabitants. This map shows how a projected sea level rise of 6.5 feet (2 meters) may affect the coastal cities of Java, an island of Indonesia.

The rising waters will push coastlines inland, but inland parts of large landmasses will not be especially affected, at least not directly. Islands, on the other hand, will be devastated. Surrounded on all sides by the ocean, many islands will shrink dramatically. Some will even disappear entirely under the water.

Vanishing islands

The nation of Indonesia consists of more than 17,500 islands, most uninhabited. Its larger islands include Java, Sumatra, and part of Borneo and New Guinea. In 2007, the country's minister for the environment warned that sea levels could cover 2,000 of its islands by 2030.

Indonesia's islands are not the only ones endangered from increasing sea levels. The president of the Maldives, a country of small, low-lying islands southwest of India, said the rising sea threatened the survival of the nation itself. If the United Nations panel's estimate of rising sea levels proves correct, much of the country would end up underwater. Most of the 1,200 small coral islands that make up the Maldives are only about 6 feet (1.8 meters) above sea level.

Dwindling fresh water

Many islands, particularly small ones, have limited freshwater supplies. On some islands, rainwater is stored in large **reservoirs.** Most small islands, however, depend on ground water.

Rising sea levels increase the threat that ground water supplies will mix with salt water, eliminating islanders' drinking source. The rock under many islands, particularly those made of coral, is porous (filled with holes), which enables water to pass through it. The higher sea levels rise, the more likely it is that salt water will contaminate small islands' drinking supplies. **Desalination**, the process by which salt is removed from sea water, is one possible solution, but it is extremely expensive.

Storm warnings

Islands in various places are especially vulnerable to **tropical cyclones**, which are storms with strong winds that form over very warm ocean water. Some scientists have predicted that a warming ocean will cause these storms to become more frequent and intense, with stronger winds and more rain.

In addition, rising sea levels could make storm surges (large waves caused by strong winds) from tropical cyclones worse. Stronger storm surges pose a special danger to low-lying islands.

A tropical cyclone killed tens of thousands of people in low-lying Myanmar in 2008.

What Are the Polar Regions?

Section Summary

The polar regions, also called the Arctic and Antarctic, are areas of bitterly cold land and ocean that lie at the North Pole and South Pole, respectively. Human interference, such as whale hunting and drilling for natural resources, threatens these ecosystems.

Global warming has caused dramatic changes to the polar regions. The melting of polar ice threatens animals in the polar regions and may also speed up global warming.

Icebergs can weigh more than 1 million tons (910,000 metric tons) and stretch for many miles.

The polar regions are the areas of bitterly cold land and ocean that lie at the northernmost and southernmost parts of Earth. They surround the North Pole and South Pole. The north polar region is the Arctic. The south polar region is the Antarctic.

The contrasting poles

The polar regions are similar in some ways but extremely different in others. Both are far colder than other parts of Earth. Both experience weeks of continuous daylight in summer, and weeks of darkness in winter. Of the two, the Antarctic is far colder. Except for Greenland, much of the land in the Arctic has no snow or ice in summer. Ice-free land areas make up only 2 percent of the Antarctic.

There is one main difference between the two polar regions: The Arctic is an ocean surrounded by continents; the Antarctic is a continent surrounded by an ocean. Much of the Arctic consists of the ice-covered Arctic Ocean, which is bordered by the northernmost coasts of Europe and North America and thousands of islands. It merges with the North Atlantic between eastern North America and western Europe, and meets the Pacific Ocean through the Bering Strait, between Siberia and Alaska.

The Antarctic, on the other hand, is a continent, Antarctica, that is surrounded by the Southern Ocean. The continent itself, almost all buried by ice, covers about 4,700,000 square miles (12,100,000 square kilometers). Europe and Australia are both smaller than Antarctica. Antarctica's interior experiences the coldest temperatures on the planet.

Boundaries of the polar regions

Scientists have different ways to mark the boundaries of the polar regions. One way is by the polar circles—the Arctic Circle and the Antarctic Circle. The Arctic Circle is an imaginary line drawn around the area in the northern hemisphere where, for at least one day each year, the sun does not set. The Antarctic Circle is a similar imaginary line in the Southern Hemisphere.

Scientists often use another imaginary boundary line for the Arctic based on temperature. This line is drawn through northern areas where the average summer temperature is 50 °F (10 °C). The line closely follows the tree line—the northernmost area in which forests can grow. Generally speaking, the Arctic includes the northern parts of Alaska, Canada, Norway, Sweden, Finland, and Russia. The Arctic also includes all of Greenland and most of Iceland.

No trees grow in Antarctica, so it does not have a similar boundary line. However, the Antarctic region was defined by a political agreement between countries with an interest in the area. The Antarctic Treaty defines this region as everything south of 60° south **latitude**, which includes the Southern Ocean.

Many scientists use a different definition of the Antarctic. Just south of 60° south latitude lies a band of water where cold southern waters sink beneath warm northern waters. This band of water, called the Antarctic Convergence, marks a natural boundary between different climates and groups of marine life. It can also be considered the region's boundary.

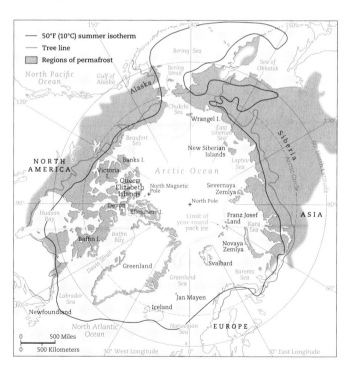

The Arctic Circle marks the edge of an area where the sun stays above the horizon one or more days each year.

The Arctic tundra stretches across the northernmost lands of Europe, Asia, and North America.

THE ARCTIC

The Arctic consists of many different environments. The Arctic Ocean, the northernmost part of the Arctic, is a treacherous landscape of drifting sea ice—that is, frozen ocean water. The ice covers most of the ocean in winter, but in summer it melts back to less than half its winter area.

Further south lie the northernmost lands of Europe, Asia, and North America. Some parts of the land, including much of Greenland, are covered in thick, frozen glaciers. The **tundra**—a treeless landscape with permanently frozen soil—stretches across many Arctic lands to the southern borders of the Arctic. There, a vast ring of evergreen forests called the taiga circles the globe, marking the tree line. Some areas of the Arctic turn into swampy bogs in summer, when some of the ice melts.

Frozen desert

Many people think of the Arctic as a place of endless, heavy snowstorms. Though it is true that snow covers the ground for much of the year, actual snowfall in the Arctic is light. The air is usually too cold to hold much moisture, so **precipitation** cannot fall. Many parts of the Arctic receive only 2 to 10 inches (5 to 25 centimeters) of precipitation each year, which is less than some deserts.

In the Arctic, the climate does not necessarily grow colder the farther north one goes. Winter temperatures on the sea ice around the North Pole average about –30 °F (–34 °C). The moderating influence of the ocean keeps temperatures from becoming even colder. In summer, temperatures around the North Pole average about 32 °F (0 °C).

The Arctic gets much colder inland, even south of the region generally defined as the Arctic. Parts of Siberia can be much colder than the average temperature on the sea ice during winter. Temperatures in Siberia can drop below –90 °F (–68 °C), especially in areas at high elevation. Temperatures also are lower in interior Greenland, which is covered by a huge ice sheet, like the ice sheets that cover Antarctica.

Sea ice

The ice that covers the Arctic Ocean melts during summer and expands in winter. The area of ice remaining in summer is considered the permanent ice pack.

Although sea ice may seem barren, it harbors plenty of life. **Plankton** grows in the water beneath and around it. Seals raise their young on the ice and are, in turn, hunted by polar bears. Arctic foxes regularly cross the ice. Sea birds hunt fish in open water around the edge of the ice pack. Even within the ice, tiny worms called nematodes (*NEHM uh tohds*) live in salty channels that never freeze. No part of the Arctic, in fact, is without life.

Sea ice may seem barren, but it supports life both above and below the surface. These seals raise their pups on the ice.

In summer, the Arctic explodes with plant life, including about 900 types of flowers.

ARCTIC PLANTS

During the long winter, it might seem as if the Arctic had no more plant life than the surface of the moon. However, many plants and plantlike organisms grow in the Arctic, even within sea ice. The ice may look lifeless, but many plankton live under and around the edges of the ice. For most of the year, the Arctic's land area may seem lifeless as well. However, hundreds of flowering plants grow on the tundra. During the winter, they lie **dormant** (in an inactive state), and their seeds wait to sprout with the thaw.

The treeless plain

Much of the Arctic landscape is tundra, consisting largely of flat, treeless land. Trees grow at the southern boundary of the Arctic at the edge of the tree line, but they reach only a few feet high.

The growing season on the tundra is extremely short, lasting only two months or less in most places. Snow covers much of the tundra until June. Tundra soil is permanently frozen, and only the top layer thaws each year during summer.

Despite these extreme conditions, the tundra explodes with plant life during the short summer. About 900 types of flowers blaze with color on the tundra during this time. Low shrubs, grasses, sedges, and mosses turn green.

Adaptations to the tundra

Arctic plants are **adapted** to withstand the bitter cold, harsh winds, and poor soil. They carry out **photosynthesis** under low light and in the cold. Many Arctic plants grow extremely slowly, often less than an inch each year. But these plants flower quickly, taking advantage of the short periods of warmth and light.

Because tundra soil is frozen except for a shallow top layer, many Arctic plants have shallow, spreading roots instead of deep roots. These shallow roots also help Arctic plants better absorb the few nutrients in tundra soil. Arctic plants often have small, tough leaves that help them store water and resist cold. They also lie low to the ground, which keeps them out of the harsh wind and blowing snow and ice. Many Arctic plants are long-lived, able to survive several growing seasons.

Lichens

Along with plants, organisms called **lichens** (*LY kuhns*) cover much of the tundra. A lichen is a combination of an alga and a fungus that grow together as if they were a single living thing. The alga uses photosynthesis to make food from sunlight. The fungus helps absorb water the alga needs to use in photosynthesis.

Many lichens grow like crusts over the ground or on bare rocks. Others, such as reindeer moss, are spongy. Despite its name, reindeer moss is actually a lichen—though it is an important food for reindeer and caribou.

Lichens are a combination of an alga and a fungus. They can grow on barren ground or even bare rock.

ARCTIC ANIMALS

As far as some animals are concerned, the Arctic is like a summer resort town. Because winter in the Arctic is so extreme, only a few animals stay year-round. But during summer, the Arctic's population explodes as a flood of visitors arrives.

Millions of birds

The most numerous summer visitors are birds. Millions of birds—mostly waterfowl, shore birds, and sea birds—nest and rear young on the shores of the Arctic. Many of them winter as far south as the tropics. They begin their journey north when the Arctic is still gripped by winter. The trip is timed so that they arrive in spring.

Millions of birds migrate to the Arctic each spring.

A few birds do stay in the Arctic throughout the winter, and their bodies adapt to the snow and cold. For example, the snowy owl and the ptarmigan (*TAHR muh guhn*) grow thick layers of feathers on their feet during winter to keep warm.

Ocean life

Because cold waters have more nutrients than warm waters, the Arctic Ocean is extremely **fertile.** When the summer brings sunlight, the Arctic Ocean explodes with **phytoplankton.** These phytoplankton feed such animals as **krill,** which provide food for larger animals, such as fish and whales. Among the Arctic's many summer visitors are whales, which feed on krill and other plankton that grow abundantly in the Arctic Ocean.

Fish, along with squid, support huge populations of Arctic seals. Like whales, seals are insulated from the cold water by a thick layer of fat called blubber.

Polar bears also depend on the Arctic Ocean and live mainly on top of its thick ice. From there, they hunt seals in the waters below. Polar bears are protected from the cold by a layer of blubber under their skin that can be up to 4 inches (10 centimeters) thick. The bears spend much of the year on the pack ice. Their feet are partially webbed, helping them swim for long distances through open water.

The Arctic fox and the polar bear are both adapted to survive Arctic temperatures.

Arctic land animals

Few land animals can survive the long Arctic winter. Cold-blooded animals, such as reptiles, amphibians, and insects, are rare in the Arctic. Because their body temperature stays the same as their surroundings, the cold winters would freeze them solid.

The wood frog of North America is an amphibian that can survive the Arctic's freezing temperatures. Its liver releases sugars throughout its body, which lowers its body's freezing point. Although the water around the frog may freeze, the frog's body can stay active. Other cold-blooded animals hibernate during winter.

Mammals, like birds, are warm-blooded animals. Mammals that live in the Arctic through winter are specially adapted to the cold. The Arctic fox has a shorter snout, legs, and ears than most foxes. These features, along with its thickly furred feet, help it **conserve** heat. Some Arctic animals, such as caribou, grow thicker fur in winter. Other animals, such as the Arctic ground squirrel, hibernate through winter.

A CLOSER LOOK
Arctic Peoples

People have lived in the Arctic for thousands of years. In the past, Arctic peoples lived in small, widely scattered groups. They moved around each year, following herds of caribou and other animals that they hunted for food. They spoke dozens of different languages.

Today, most native Arctic peoples have settled in modern towns. They drive snowmobiles or all-terrain vehicles across the snowy landscapes. Many speak English or other European languages instead of their native languages, which are in danger of dying out. Rapid modernization has caused social problems in some native communities.

Ice fishing has been a part of Arctic people's culture for more than 1,000 years.

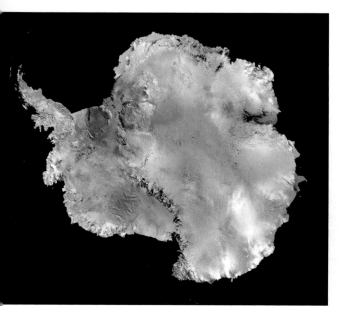

THE ANTARCTIC

The Antarctic continent covers about 4,700,000 square miles (12,100,000 square kilometers). About 98 percent of the continent is covered by an ice sheet that averages about 7,100 feet (2,200 meters) in thickness. Even though Antarctica receives very little precipitation, the snow that does fall has built up over thousands of years to form this towering ice sheet, which flows outward from the middle of the continent. At the shorelines, the ice extends far out into the ocean as ice shelves. The ice shelves continually break off as icebergs, but they regrow as they receive ice from inland.

Larger than Europe, Antarctica is the coldest, most barren place on Earth.

Ice world

Antarctica's vast ice sheet contains 90 percent of the world's ice and 70 percent of its fresh water. If it melted, the **world ocean** would rise 230 feet (70 meters), flooding most coastal cities. The weight of the ice in the interior causes it to spread toward the coast. Ice near the coast moves as much as 660 feet (200 meters) each year. Glaciers flow through Antarctica's narrow valleys even faster. The weight of the ice also presses down on the land underneath, causing much of it to sink below sea level.

Only a few ice-free areas exist in Antarctica, covering about 2 percent of the continent. Deep in the interior, dry valleys lie between mountains where wind has swept away the snow. The largest of these is a 1,853-square-mile (4,800-square-kilometer) expanse along the western coast of McMurdo Sound. A fringe of coastal areas, particularly on the Antarctic Peninsula, is also free of ice.

Temperature and weather

Antarctica is the coldest region on Earth. The Antarctic summer is short, lasting only from mid-December to mid-January in the middle of the continent, and longer along the coasts. The annual average temperature in the interior is −58 °F (−50 °C), but it gets much colder than that. Winter lows of −94 °F (−70 °C) are not uncommon. Interior temperatures even in summer seldom go above 5 °F (–15 °C). However, summer temperatures on the Antarctic Peninsula often rise above freezing, occasionally even reaching 59 °F (15 °C).

Antarctica's winds can be fierce, both in the center of the continent and on the Antarctic Peninsula. Winds blowing from the high plateau can average 44 miles (70 kilometers) an hour. These winds are often generated by cold, heavy air that falls quickly toward the ground and spreads outward. When these winds reach the coast, they drive the formation and spread of sea ice. Coastal gusts often blow at 120 miles (190 kilometers) an hour. One spot along the coast, Cape Dennison, is known as the windiest spot on Earth. Its strongest winds reach 185 miles (300 kilometers) per hour.

Although Antarctica is blanketed in snow, it is—like parts of the Arctic—actually drier than many deserts. The snow that falls here never melts, so it stays on the ground or gets pressed into the ice sheet. Annual snowfall on the inland plateau of ice is only about 2 inches (5 centimeters). On the coast, it averages 24 inches (61 centimeters).

Only a few ice-free areas exist in Antarctica, 98 percent of which is covered by ice.

The abundant ocean life around Antarctica supports large animals, such as this crabeater seal.

ANTARCTIC PLANTS AND ANIMALS

Although Antarctica is sometimes described as a lifeless continent, it is home to some of the largest living things on Earth, as well as some of the smallest. As scientists continue to explore the region, they find an increasing variety of organisms that live there.

Life in miniature

Lying in the windswept dry valleys of the interior are ice-covered lakes. Beneath the ice, scientists have found microscopic phytoplankton and several types of bacteria. The largest organisms in the valleys are worms called nematodes.

Scientists have also found bacteria and algae in the upper levels of Antarctica's ice sheet. These organisms remain in an inactive state for most of the year. However, when the summer sun melts small amounts of the ice sheet's surface, they become active and quickly reproduce.

Giants

Antarctica is also home to giant organisms that live in the Southern Ocean. They include the blue whale, the largest animal that has ever lived. Other whales also migrate to the Southern Ocean to feed on krill.

Whales are not the only giant organisms in the Southern Ocean. In 2008, scientists in Antarctica's Ross Sea reported that they had found a jellyfish with 12-foot- (3.7-meter-) long tentacles and sea stars 2 feet (0.6 meters) across. During a 50-day exploration of the sea, the scientists found large numbers of other **invertebrates.**

Lack of land life

Only two flowering plants grow on Antarctica, both on the Antarctic Peninsula. One is a low grass. The other is a cushion-like herb.

No large land animals spend their entire lives on the frozen continent. Penguins do live on the land, but they also hunt in the sea. The largest animal that lives only on the continent is the wingless midge, a type of fly only half an inch (12 millimeters) long. A few ticks, mites, and lice cling to the fur of seals, the feathers of birds, and mosses.

Abundant sea life

Penguins breed on Antarctica's land, but they rely on the sea for food. Protected by dense, waterproof feathers and a thick layer of blubber, they dive swiftly into the cold waters and hunt for fish. Four kinds of penguins breed on Antarctica—the emperor, Adélie, chinstrap, and gentoo penguins. The king penguin breeds on islands at the fringes of Antarctica. Emperor penguins breed inland, huddling together for warmth.

Emperor penguins breed on Antarctica's land, though they are dependent on the ocean for food.

The ocean around the Antarctic abounds with sea life. Crabeater seals, Weddell seals, Ross seals, and several other seals live there. Killer whales hunt seals, other whales, and penguins. Along with killer whales, one of the fiercest predators of penguins is the leopard seal. These spotted hunters lie in wait along the edges of ice or rocks from which penguins dive into the water. They can lurch onto the ice to grab unsuspecting birds. Leopard seals have even attacked people, though such attacks are extremely rare.

In summer, more than 40 species of sea birds nest on the shores of Antarctica and its offshore islands. Several of these, such as petrels and shearwaters, spend almost their entire lives over the ocean. Others are species that remain in coastal waters, including skuas, gulls, and terns. All told, perhaps 100 million birds breed along the Antarctic's shores.

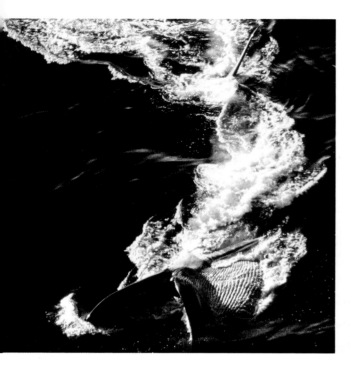

WHALES AND WHALING

Krill—tiny shrimplike organisms—are plentiful in the Southern Ocean. Masses of krill covering 174 square miles (450 square kilometers) have been observed in Antarctic waters. Krill feed on phytoplankton, which grow abundantly in the Southern Ocean's nutritious waters.

The krill, in turn, provide food for Earth's largest organisms—whales. Blue whales and other whales use the Southern Ocean as a summer feeding ground. These whales do not have teeth. Instead, their mouths are equipped with large, fringed plates called **baleen.** They swim through masses of krill, swallowing huge amounts of the tiny animals, and then strain out the water through the baleen.

The blue whale is the largest animal that has ever lived. It feeds on tiny krill.

Whales in danger

Despite the Southern Ocean's abundance of food, many whales are on the brink of extinction. Whales were hunted relentlessly throughout the 1800's and 1900's. With several species almost extinct, several countries formed the International Whaling Commission (IWC) to conserve endangered whale populations. In 1982, the IWC succeeded in ordering a halt to **commercial** whaling. Today, nearly 80 countries are members of the IWC.

However, not all countries agreed with the whaling ban. A few—notably Norway and Iceland—continue to hunt whales commercially in a limited way. Other countries, especially Japan, kill whales for what their governments claim are scientific purposes—although whale meat still ends up in markets and restaurants. All told, about 30,000 whales have been killed since 1985, when the commercial whaling ban went into effect.

Not all whales are in danger. The Pacific gray whale population has recovered to numbers not seen since before large-scale whaling began. However, six types of baleen whales are protected under the United States Endangered Species Act—blue, bowhead, fin, humpback, right, and sei (*say*) whales. As marine mammals, whales are also protected in the United States by the federal Marine Mammal Protection Act.

GREEN FACT

In 1994, the International Whaling Commission established the Southern Ocean Whale Sanctuary. This sanctuary covers most of the world's oceans that lie south of 40° south latitude.

Why whales are hunted

Whale oil was once one of the world's most important commercial oils. It was used for **varnish**, making soap and leather, and lighting. Lamps burning whale oil lighted much of the world for centuries. Oil and other whale products are no longer imported, except in a few countries where they are an accepted part of culture. This is true in Japan, where almost every part of the whale is used for one type of product or another—from food to **pesticides.** For this reason, many Japanese people have a different view of whaling than people in nations that do not use whale products.

Stopping whaling

Environmentalists believe that whales cannot survive any more pressure from commercial whaling. Even though some whale populations have recovered, all are threatened by human activities. According to the U.S. Commission on Ocean Policy, 300,000 whales and their smaller relatives, dolphins and porpoises, die as **bycatch** in fishing nets each year. Warming of the oceans may also endanger whales.

Environmentalists continue to fight to stop all whaling, including whaling that governments claim is for scientific purposes. They also aim to create international agreements that establish ocean sanctuaries in which whales are completely protected from people. In 1994, the IWC established the largest whale sanctuary in the world around Antarctica, though scientific whaling still kills hundreds of whales there each year.

Greenpeace, an environmental organization, has sometimes confronted Japanese whaling ships.

The Arctic Coastal Plain is home to both the Arctic National Wildlife Refuge and the Prudhoe Bay oil fields, shown above.

INDUSTRIALIZATION AND DEVELOPMENT

The Arctic is the focus of ongoing controversy between environmentalists and those who want to use its resources. The Arctic contains many natural resources, such as minerals, natural gas, and oil. The Antarctic is less controversial because international agreements currently prohibit mining and other development on that continent.

Environmental issues

The U.S. State Department describes the nation's policy toward the Arctic as trying to balance environmental protection and development. Often, government approaches to dealing with the Arctic environment satisfy no one. Environmentalists complain that the environment and the wildlife it supports are being sacrificed for new oil and gas development. Supporters of drilling say that wildlife sanctuaries prevent removal of natural resources that are critical to economic survival.

Some conservation groups are taking the middle ground. They try to find ways that Arctic resources can be reasonably developed while protecting the environment. Since 2002, for instance, the Wildlife Conservation Society (WCS) has been studying how oil development affects the nesting of shore birds that breed in Alaska. They study the effects of oil development on wildlife in hopes of determining areas that need full protection.

Arctic Coastal Plain

Much of the controversy is centered on the Arctic Coastal Plain, where the WCS concentrates its studies. The plain edges the coast of the Arctic Ocean in Canada's Northwest Territories and Alaska. Its key area is called the Alaskan North Slope, which lies on the northern end of the Brooks Range, a mountain range that stretches west to east across northern Alaska.

The Arctic National Wildlife Refuge, the only protected Arctic coastline in the United States, lies in this area. It is also the site of the Prudhoe Bay oil fields and the National Petroleum Reserve-Alaska. The reserve was established in 1923 as a future source of oil for the nation. Like the rest of the North Slope, it teems with wildlife such as caribou, wolves, shore birds, water birds, and grizzly bears. In what seems like an endless battle, environmentalists and oil-development interests argue over the reserve's future.

Many threats

In addition to harming the environment, development in the Arctic also threatens the livelihood of the human beings who have lived there for centuries. The removal of minerals, natural gas, and oil from Arctic lands has damaged hunting and fishing in many areas. Rapid modernization in the Arctic has brought many benefits to people living there, but it has also led to many social problems in traditional Arctic communities.

Development is only one of the potential threats to the polar environment. Scientists now must consider not only the impact of development, but of such forces as **global warming.** Polar bears, for instance, could be in danger from oil spills and the disturbance caused by the drilling and transport of oil. At the same time, shrinking sea ice threatens them.

The Trans-Alaska oil pipeline stretches across hundreds of miles of wilderness.

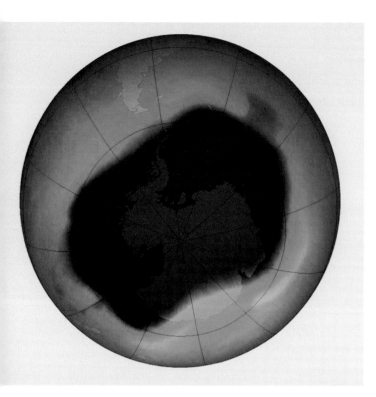

The hole in the ozone layer allows ultraviolet rays from the sun to reach Earth's surface, threatening life.

THE OZONE HOLE

Ozone is a gas that is naturally part of Earth's **atmosphere.** It has been disappearing from the atmosphere over Antarctica, which is very bad news for living things on Earth.

What is ozone?

One **molecule** of ozone is made when three oxygen **atoms** stick together. When ozone is close to the surface of Earth, it acts as a **pollutant.** (For more information on ozone pollution, see the "Closer Look" sidebar on page 55.) Most ozone, however, exists naturally far above the surface of Earth. At this height, ozone actually protects living things on Earth. It forms a layer that blocks harmful **ultraviolet rays** from the sun.

Some radiation from the sun is beneficial. It helps the human body form vitamin D. However, it also causes sunburn and skin cancer. Most life could not exist if large amounts of the sun's radiation hit Earth. The ozone layer in the atmosphere is thus essential to life on Earth.

The ozone hole

Ozone is not an abundant gas. Even in the ozone layer high above Earth, there are only around 1,200 ozone molecules for every billion molecules of air. If all atmospheric ozone were brought down to Earth's surface and spread out, it would form a layer less than 0.25 inches (0.6 centimeters) thick.

Scarce as it is, ozone has been vanishing. In the late 1970's, scientists discovered that the amount of ozone in the atmosphere over Antarctica was dropping from August through November, which is late winter to early spring there. This was the first sign of what now is known as the Antarctic ozone hole. At times, it has covered more than 11 million square miles (28.5 million square kilometers).

Scientists found that the loss of ozone came largely from chemicals produced by humans. Those with the greatest impact

The United States launched the Aura satellite in 2004 to monitor changes in the ozone layer.

Ozone gas occurs naturally high in the atmosphere, where it protects Earth from ultraviolet rays. But in the lowest level of the atmosphere, ozone is a human-made pollutant and the main ingredient of urban **smog.** Ground-level ozone is formed by gases called **nitrogen oxides** and **volatile organic compounds (VOC's),** which are released by vehicles, power plants, and factories. When sunlight strikes nitrogen oxides and VOC's, they form ozone. As a consequence, ozone pollution is usually worse during summer days. Ozone pollution can cause respiratory problems. It also damages plants, such as trees and food crops.

are called **chlorofluorocarbons** (*KLAWR uh FLOOR uh KAHR buhns*) or **CFC's.** These compounds contain chlorine, fluorine, and carbon, which break down ozone in the upper atmosphere. CFC's were once widely used as a propellant for aerosol cans and as a refrigerant and insulator.

CFC's are not particularly concentrated in the Antarctic. Ozone is thinning in other areas as well. The problem is greatest at the South Pole because cold temperatures there quicken the loss of ozone.

Solving the problem

In one of the few environmental success stories of modern times, the ozone layer is expected to recover by the middle of this century. The reason for this is a landmark international agreement signed in 1987 called the Montreal Protocol, which phased out the use of chemicals that have thinned the ozone layer. However, scientists warn that the ozone layer's recovery could be slowed if there were an unusual outbreak of volcanic eruptions, which release gases that can also deplete ozone gas. Another force that could harm the ozone layer is global warming.

Smog in Mexico City

Some polar bears have drowned while swimming across long stretches of open ocean that were once covered with sea ice.

CLIMATE CHANGE AND THE POLAR REGIONS

Over the past few decades, scientists have observed the polar regions as evidence of global warming in action. These regions are currently some of the areas most visibly affected by climate change.

Shrinking sea ice

Arctic sea ice in the summer of 2007 covered a record low of 1.65 million square miles (4.28 million square kilometers). It was down 23 percent from a previous record low just two years before. Moreover, the thickness of the Arctic sea ice is also decreasing.

Melting Arctic sea ice could harm polar bear populations along the Arctic Ocean. The polar bears use the sea ice as platforms from which they hunt seals in the water beneath. Without sea ice, many polar bears would starve.

The situation in the Antarctic is less clear. Some studies show the sea ice there is decreasing. Others show that it is increasing, and still others indicate that it may be stable.

Glaciers and ice shelves

The melting of sea ice does not raise Earth's sea level, because the sea ice was originally part of the ocean. However, melting freshwater glaciers and ice sheets that cover polar lands would cause an increase in the sea level. These ice sheets also seem to be shrinking from global warming. In Greenland, the melting has more than doubled since 2000. Small islands that were once covered by Greenland's glacier are now appearing just offshore.

Antarctica's vast glacial ice shelves are falling apart at the edges as well. In early 2008, scientists were startled when satellite images showed a huge chunk of ice had broken off from Antarctica's Wilkins Ice Shelf. The shelf is a 5,000-square-mile (12,966-square-kilometer) plate of ice floating at the edge of the continent. The piece that fell off measured 160 square miles (414 square kilometers). Scientists worried that additional collapses could send the entire ice shelf crashing into the sea.

A vicious circle

If sea levels rise, land inhabited by millions of people—from the lowlands of southern Asia to the great cities of Europe and North America—could be flooded.

Disappearing ice covers in polar lands could have another disastrous effect. Ice and snow reflect the sun's heat, just as white summer clothing does. The shiny white ice cover on the Arctic Ocean helps to keep down temperatures. The darker waters of an open ocean, on the other hand, absorb heat and raise temperatures. This means that as more polar ice melts, global warming might speed up, and the rest of the ice could melt even faster.

Taking action

People around the world have called for governments to take action in order to limit global warming. Reducing **carbon dioxide** emissions from cars, factories, and power plants is essential to doing so. Investing in alternative forms of energy, such as wind and solar (sun) power and **biofuels**, could help stop global warming from spiraling out of control. Many scientists warn that actions must be taken immediately in order to prevent Earth's ecosystems from being irreparably harmed.

These two images show the Grinnell Glacier in North America in 1940 (bottom left) and 2006 (bottom right). Ice melt has dramatically decreased the size of the glacier.

Activities

ECO-ACTION AT HOME

Protecting Earth's **ecosystems** starts with implementing environmentally friendly practices at home and in your community. Here are a few things you can do to help keep Earth green:

- Reduce waste by choosing long-lasting items over disposable goods (goods that are thrown away immediately after use).

- Recycle metal, glass, paper, and plastic items to help save energy and reduce **fossil fuel emissions.** Start a recycling program at school if one doesn't already exist.

- Organize cleanup days in your neighborhood or at a local park.

- Reduce the amount of water you use. Turn off the faucet when cleaning dishes or brushing your teeth, and take quick showers.

- Avoid using chemical **pesticides** and **fertilizers** in your garden or yard.

- Replace standard light bulbs with compact fluorescent light bulbs (CFL's), which are energy efficient.

- Instead of driving a car, walk, ride your bike, or take public transportation whenever possible.

RESEARCH PROJECT: INVASIVE SPECIES

Introduction

Invasive species wreak havoc on ecosystems and have caused much damage to ocean and island environments. Learn more about invasive species around the world or in your region.

The Invasive Species Specialist Group is an organization that works to raise awareness of invasive species and the threats they pose to ecosystems throughout the world. You can visit their Web site to look up invasive species in your area. You can also view a list of the 100 worst invasive species, ranging from plants to insects and other animals.
http://www.issg.org/database/welcome/

Directions:

1. Research one of the following invasive species, or choose your own:
   - Brown tree snake (*Boiga irregularis*)
   - Comb jellyfish (*Mnemiopsis leidyi*)
   - Zebra mussels (*Dreissena polymorpha*)
   - Macartney rose (*Rosa bracteata*)

2. Ask your school librarian to help you find information on your invasive species. Together, come up with a list of things you'd like to find out about this species. Examples of such questions include:
   - Where did the species originate?
   - How was it introduced to other environments?
   - Where does it live in the world today?
   - What damage has it caused to these ecosystems?
   - How are people working to control the harmful effects of this species?

3. Create a report that gives important information about the invasive species. The report could be in the form of a booklet, poster, collage, blog, podcast, or a combination of media.

Zebra mussels, a shellfish native to Asia, have caused many problems in the United States, especially in the Great Lakes.

Glossary

abyssal plain a vast, flat plain at the bottom of ocean basins.

adapt to make fit or suitable; adjust.

algal bloom a sudden, abnormal explosion of the population of algae in a body of water caused by large amounts of nutrients in the water.

atmosphere the mixture of gases in contact with Earth's surface and extending far above.

atoll a ring-shaped coral island or group of islands enclosing or partly enclosing a lagoon.

atom the smallest particle of a chemical element that can take part in a chemical reaction without being permanently changed.

baleen plates that grow downward from the upper jaws or palates of certain whales.

biofuel a liquid fuel made from plant matter, animal waste, or other biological sources.

bycatch fish and other marine animals inadvertently caught by fishing boats that cannot be sold.

by-product an additional product created in the manufacture of an object or substance.

camouflage protective coloration that helps animals hide from predators.

carbon dioxide a colorless, odorless gas given off by burning and by animals breathing out.

chlorofluorocarbons (CFC's) human-made chemicals that cause ozone in the atmosphere to disappear.

commercial having to do with trade or business.

conserve; conservation to keep from harm or loss; the management, protection, and wise use of natural resources.

continental shelf a shallow, gently sloped area of the ocean floor connected to the continents.

coral bleaching the whitening of coral due to the loss of algae that live within the tissue of polyps.

countershading protective coloring characterized by the relatively darker coloration of an animal's exposed parts and lighter coloration of its shaded parts.

dead zone an area in the ocean with too little oxygen for plant and animal life to survive.

desalination the process of removing salt from salt water such as ocean water.

diatom any one of numerous microscopic, one-celled, aquatic algae.

dormant in plants, a period during which growth processes stop, enabling them to survive during cold or dry weather.

ecosystem a group of interrelated living things and the environment on which they depend.

emission an airborne waste product.

environmentalist a person who wants to preserve nature and reduce pollution.

erosion gradual wearing away by wind, rain, ice, or other forces.

evaporate to change from a liquid or solid into a vapor or gas.

fertile able to support growth.

fertilizer a substance that helps plants to grow.

food chain a group of interrelated organisms in which each member of the group feeds upon the one below it and is in turn eaten by the organism above it.

fossil fuel underground deposits that were formed millions of years ago from the remains of plants and animals. Coal, oil, and natural gas are fossil fuels.

global warming the gradual warming of Earth's surface, believed to be caused by a build-up of greenhouse gases in the atmosphere.

greenhouse effect the process by which certain gases cause the Earth's atmosphere to warm.

greenhouse gas any gas that contributes to the greenhouse effect.

ground water water that pools underground in porous rocks.

habitat the place where an animal or plant naturally lives or grows.

hydrothermal vent a place where hot, often nutrient-rich water flows up from beneath the ocean floor.

ice age any one of several periods in Earth's history when ice sheets covered a great deal of land.

invasive species a living thing that is transported to a new environment where it spreads rapidly and threatens local wildlife.

invertebrate an animal without a backbone.

kelp a variety of large seaweeds that grow underwater and on rocky shores.

krill tiny, shrimplike organisms that live near the surface of the ocean.

latitude the distance north or south of the equator, measured in degrees.

lichen an organism consisting of an alga and a fungus, growing together on rocks, trees, or other surfaces.

limestone a type of rock made mostly of the chemical compound calcium carbonate.

marine snow bits of dead organisms from surface waters that fall to the deep ocean and supply food for animals that live there.

molecule the smallest particle into which a substance can be divided without a chemical change.

nitrogen oxide a compound of nitrogen and oxygen.

ocean basin the portion of the ocean beyond the continental shelf; most of the ocean.

ozone a form of oxygen gas.

permafrost permanently frozen soil.

pesticide a poison that kills pests, such as insects.

photic zone the sunlit surface waters of the ocean, extending about 330 feet (100 meters) deep.

photosynthesis the process by which plant cells make energy from sunlight.

phytoplankton tiny plantlike organisms that float in the oceans and use the sun's energy to make food.

plankton tiny organisms that thrive in the sunlit surface waters of the ocean.

pollutant a single source of pollution.

polyp a small, soft relative of jellyfish and sea anemones, with a hollow, tubelike body rimmed by tentacles.

precipitation rain, snow, sleet, ice, or hail.

refinery a factory in which useful products such as gasoline are extracted from crude oil.

regulate to control by rule, principle, or system.

reservoir a pond or lake formed by a dam.

salinity the amount of salt concentrated in the water.

sewage water that contains waste matter produced by human beings.

silt fine grains of soil, rock or similar materials washed off land into bodies of water.

smog a brown, hazy mixture of gases and particulates caused by exhaust gases released by automobiles and other users of fossil fuels.

tectonic plate a ridged piece of earth on the outermost layer of Earth's crust. Tectonic plates move on top of a layer of hot rock called magma.

tropical cyclone a storm with strong winds and rain that forms in warm, humid air over warm ocean water.

tundra cold, dry, treeless lands of the Arctic.

ultraviolet rays the invisible rays in the part of the spectrum beyond the violet.

United Nations an international organization that works for world peace and human prosperity.

varnish a liquid used to protect wood, metal, and other materials and to improve their appearance.

volatile organic compounds (VOC's) an unstable substance that breaks down over time and gives off small amounts of toxic gases.

world ocean the five oceans of Earth—the Atlantic, Pacific, Indian, Southern, and Arctic oceans—taken together.

zooplankton tiny animals and animallike organisms that float in the sunlit surface waters of the ocean.

Additional Resources

WEB SITES

Canadian Environmental Assessment Agency
http://www.ceaa-acee.gc.ca

Provides environmental assessments that contribute to well-informed decision making.

Earth 911
http://www.earth911.org

An environmental organization that urges people to make every day Earth Day; includes a student section.

Environment Agency
http://www.environment-agency.gov.uk

Provides tools to make the environment a better place for you and for future generations; includes resources for schools.

Friends of the Earth
http://www.foe.co.uk

Offers inspiring solutions to the world's environmental problems.

National Geographic
http://www.nationalgeographic.com

Features articles, video, and photography of environmental issues around the world; includes a student section with games and activities.

National Oceanic and Atmospheric Administration
http://www.noaa.gov

Includes information on many science topics.

Natural Resources Defense Council
http://www.nrdc.org

Contains the latest information on ways people are working toward environmentally friendly practices.

Sierra Club
http://www.sierraclub.org

Offers information on a range of environmental issues.

United States Environmental Protection Agency
http://www.epa.gov

Much information on pollution and the environment; includes a student page.

BOOKS

An Extreme Dive Under the Antarctic Ice
by Brad Metson (Enslow, 2003)

Endangered Oceans: Opposing Viewpoints
by William Dudley (Editor) (Greenhaven Press, 1999)

Endangered Planet
by David Burnie and Tony Juniper (Kingfisher, 2007)

Oceans
by Trevor Day (Facts on File, Inc. 2007)

Polar Regions: Human Impacts
by Dana Desonie (Facts on File, 2008)

Index